Marx Hardy Abbott Defoe Melville Montaigne Machiavelli Haggard Chesterton Cooper Emerson Joyce Austen Hugo Eliot Grimm Molière Stoker Carroll Christie Maupassant Byron Schiller Wilde Garnett Einstein Fitzgerald Hawthorne Engels Smith Kafka Goethe Dostoyevsky Cotton Kipling Doyle Hall Willis Baum Henry Nietzsche Leslie Dumas Flaubert Turgenev Balzac Stockton Vatsyayana Crane Burroughs Verne Curtis Tocqueville Vinci Homer Widger Tolstoy Gogol Busch Darwin Thoreau Whitman Potter Freud Zola Lawrence Twain Scott Plato Harte Kant Jowett Stevenson Dickens Burton Hesse Andersen Descartes Cervantes London Poe Aristotle Wells Voltaire Cooke Hale James Hastings Bunner Shakespeare Irving Richter Chambers da Benedict Alcott Doré Dante Chekhov Shaw Wodehouse Pushkin Swift Newton

Memoirs of Louis XIV and His Court and of the Regency — Volume 03

Charlotte-Elisabeth, duchesse d' Orleans

Imprint

This book is part of TREDITION CLASSICS

Author: Charlotte-Elisabeth, duchesse d' Orleans
Cover design: Buchgut, Berlin – Germany

Publisher: tredition GmbH, Hamburg - Germany
ISBN: 978-3-8424-5345-6

www.tredition.com
www.tredition.de

MEMOIRS OF THE COURT OF LOUIS XIV. AND OF THE REGENCY

Being the Secret Memoirs of the Mother of the Regent,
MADAME ELIZABETH-CHARLOTTE OF BAVARIA, DUCHESSE
D'ORLEANS.

BOOK 3.

SECTION XVII.—HENRIETTA OF ENGLAND, THE FIRST WIFE OF MONSIEUR, BROTHER OF LOUIS XIV.

It is true that the late Madame was extremely unhappy; she confided too much in people who betrayed her: she was more to be pitied than blamed, being connected with very wicked persons, about whom I could give some particulars. Young, pretty and gay, she was surrounded by some of the greatest coquettes in the world, the mistresses of her bitterest foes, and who sought only to thrust her into some unfortunate situation and to embroil her with Monsieur. Madame de Coetquen was the Chevalier de Lorraine's mistress, although Madame did not know it; and she contrived that the Marechal de Turenne should become attached to her. Madame having told the Marshal all her secrets respecting the negotiations with England, he repeated them to his mistress, Madame de Coetquen, whom he believed to be devoted to his mistress. This woman went every night to the Chevalier de Lorraine and betrayed them all. The Chevalier used this opportunity to stir up Monsieur's indignation against Madame, telling him that he passed with the King for a simpleton, who could not hold his tongue; that he would lose all confidence, and that his wife would have everything in her own hand. Monsieur wished to know all the particulars from Madame; but she refused to tell him her brother's secrets, and this widened the breach between them. She became enraged, and had the Chevalier de Lorraine and his brother driven away, which in the end cost her own life; she, however, died with the consciousness of never having done her husband any harm. She was the confidante of the King, to whom it had been hinted that it might be expedient to give some employment to Monsieur, who might otherwise make himself beloved in the Court and in the city. For this reason the King assisted Madame in her affairs of gallantry, in order to occupy his brother. I have this from the King himself. Madame was besides in great credit with her brother, Charles II. (of England). Louis XIV. wished to gain him over through his sister, wherefore it was necessary to take part with her, and she was always better treated than I have been. The late Monsieur never suspected his wife of infidelity with the King, her brother-in-law, he told me, all her life, and would not have been silent with respect to this intrigue if he had believed it. I think that with respect to this great injustice is done to Madame. It would have been too much to deceive at once the brother and the nephew, the father and the son.

The late Monsieur was very much disturbed at his wife's coquetry; but he dared not behave ill to her, because she was protected by the King.

The Queen-mother of England had not brought up her children well: she at first left them in the society of femmes de chambre, who gratified all their caprices; and having afterwards married them at a very early age, they followed the bad example of their mother. Both of them met with unhappy deaths; the one was poisoned, and the other died in child-birth.

Monsieur was himself the cause of Madame's intrigue with the Comte de Guiche. He was one of the favourites of the late Monsieur, and was said to have been handsome once. Monsieur earnestly requested Madame to shew some favour to the Comte de Guiche, and to permit him to wait upon her at all times. The Count, who was brutal to every one else, but full of vanity, took great pains to be agreeable to Madame, and to make her love him. In fact, he succeeded, being seconded by his aunt, Madame de Chaumont, who was the gouvernante of Madame's children. One day Madame went to this lady's chamber, under the pretence of seeing her children, but in fact to meet De Guiche, with whom she had an assignation. She had a valet de chambre named Launois, whom I have since seen in the service of Monsieur; he had orders to stand sentinel on the staircase, to give notice in case Monsieur should approach. This Launois suddenly ran into the room, saying, "Monsieur is coming downstairs."

The lovers were terrified to death. The Count could not escape by the antechamber on account of Monsieur's people who were there. Launois said, "I know a way, which I will put into practice immediately; hide yourself," he said to the Count, "behind the door." He then ran his head against Monsieur's nose as he was entering, and struck him so violently that he began to bleed. At the same moment he cried out, "I beg your pardon, Monsieur, I did not think you were so near, and I ran to open you the door."

Madame and Madame de Chaumont ran in great alarm to Monsieur, and covered his face with their handkerchiefs, so that the Comte de Guiche had time to get out of the room, and escape by the staircase. Monsieur saw some one run away, but he thought it was Launois, who was escaping through fear. He never learnt the truth.

What convinces me of the late Madame's innocence is that, after having received the last sacraments, she begged pardon of Monsieur for all disquiets she had occasioned, and said that she hoped to reach heaven because she had committed no crime against her husband.

I think M. de Monmouth was much worse than the Comte de Guiche; because, although a bastard, he was the son of Madame's own brother; and this incest doubled the crime. Madame de Thiange, sister of Madame de Montespan, conducted the intrigue between the Duke of Monmouth and Madame.

It is said here that Madame was not a beauty, but that she had so graceful a manner as to make all she did very agreeable. She never forgave. She would have the Chevalier de Lorraine dismissed; he was so, but he was amply revenged of her. He sent the poison by which she was destroyed from Italy by a nobleman of Provence, named Morel: this man was afterwards given to me as chief maitre d'hotel, and after he had sufficiently robbed me they made him sell his place at a high price. This Morel was very clever, but he was a man totally void of moral or religious principle; he confessed to me that he did not believe in anything. At the point of death he would not hear talk of God. He said, speaking of himself, "Let this carcass alone, it is now good for nothing." He would steal, lie and swear; he was an atheist and.....

....

It is too true that the late Madame was poisoned, but without the knowledge of Monsieur. While the villains were arranging the plan of poisoning the poor lady, they deliberated whether they should acquaint Monsieur with it or not. The Chevalier de Lorraine said

"No, don't tell him, for he cannot hold his tongue. If he does not tell it the first year he may have us hanged ten years afterwards;" and it is well known that the wretches said, "Let us not tell Monsieur, for he would tell the King, who would certainly hang us all." They therefore made Monsieur believe that Madame had taken poison in Holland, which did not act until she arrived here.

> [It is said that the King sent for the maitre d'hotel, and that, being satisfied that Monsieur had not been a party to the crime, he said, "Then I am relieved; you may retire." The Memoirs of the day state also that the King employed the Chevalier de Lorraine to persuade Monsieur to obey his brother's wishes.]

It appears, therefore, that the wicked Gourdon took no part in this affair; but she certainly accused Madame to Monsieur, and calumniated and disparaged her to everybody.

It was not Madame's endive-water that D'Effial had poisoned; that report must have been a mere invention, for other persons might have tasted it had Madame alone drank from her own glass. A valet de chambre who was with Madame, and who afterwards was in my service (he is dead now), told me that in the morning, while Monsieur and Madame were at Mass, D'Effial went to the sideboard and, taking the Queen's cup, rubbed the inside of it with a paper. The valet said to him, "Monsieur, what do you do in this room, and why do you touch Madame's cup?" He answered, "I am dying with thirst; I wanted something to drink, and the cup being dirty, I was wiping it with some paper." In the afternoon Madame asked for some endive-water; but no sooner had she swallowed it than she exclaimed she was poisoned. The persons present drank some of the same water, but not the same that was in the cup, for which reason they were not inconvenienced by it. It was found necessary to carry Madame to bed. She grew worse, and at two o'clock in the morning she died in great pain. When the cup was sought for it had disappeared, and was not found until long after. It seems it had been necessary to pass it through the fire before it could be cleaned.

A report prevailed at St. Cloud for several years that the ghost of the late Madame appeared near a fountain where she had been accustomed to sit during the great heats, for it was a very cool spot. One evening a servant of the Marquis de Clerambault, having gone thither to draw water from the fountain, saw something white sitting there without a head. The phantom immediately arose to double its height. The poor servant fled in great terror, and said when he entered the house that he had seen Madame. He fell sick and died. Then the captain of the Chateau, thinking there was something hidden beneath this affair, went to the fountain some days afterwards, and, seeing the phantom, he threatened it with a sound drubbing if it did not declare what it was.

The phantom immediately said, "Ah, M. de Lastera, do me no harm; I am poor old Philipinette."

This was an old woman in the village, seventy-seven years old, who had lost her teeth, had blear eyes, a great mouth and large nose; in short, was a very hideous figure. They were going to take her to prison, but I interceded for her. When she came to thank me I asked her what fancy it was that had induced her to go about playing the ghost instead of sleeping.

She laughed and said, "I cannot much repent what I have done. At my time of life one sleeps little; but one wants something to amuse one's mind. In all the sports of my youth nothing diverted me so much as to play the ghost. I was very sure that if I could not frighten folks with my white dress I could do so with my ugly face. The cowards made so many grimaces when they saw it that I was ready to die with laughing. This nightly amusement repaid me for the trouble of carrying a pannier by day."

If the late Madame was better treated than I was it was for the purpose of pleasing the King of England, who was very fond of his sister.

....

Madame de La Fayette, who has written the life of the late Madame, was her intimate friend; but she was still more intimately the friend of M. de La Rochefoucauld, who remained with her to the day of his death. It is said that these two friends wrote together the romance of the Princesse de Cloves.

SECTION XVIII.—THE DUC DE BERRI.

It is not surprising that the manners of the Duc de Berri were not very elegant, since he was educated by Madame de Maintenon and the Dauphine as a valet de chambre. He was obliged to wait upon the old woman at table, and at all other times upon the Dauphine's ladies, with whom he was by day and night. They made a mere servant of him, and used to talk to him in a tone of very improper familiarity, saying, "Berri, go and fetch me my work; bring me that table; give me my scissors."

Their manner of behaving to him was perfectly shameful. This had the effect of degrading his disposition, and of giving him base propensities; so that it is not surprising he should have been violently in love with an ugly femme de chambre. His good father was naturally of rather a coarse disposition.

But for that old Maintenon, the Duc de Berri would have been humpbacked, like the rest who had been made to carry iron crosses.

The Duc de Berri's character seemed to undergo a total change; it is said to be the ordinary lot of the children in Paris that, if they display any sense in their youth, they become stupid as they grow older.

It was in compliance with the King's will that he married. At first he was passionately fond of his wife; but at the end of three months he fell in love with a little, ugly, black femme de chambre. The Duchess, who had sufficient penetration, was not slow in discovering this, and told her husband immediately that, if he continued to live upon good terms with her, as he had done at first, she would say nothing about it, and act as if she were not acquainted with it; but if he behaved ill, she would tell the whole affair to the King, and have the femme de chambre sent away, so that he should never hear of her again. By this threat she held the Duke, who was a very simple man, so completely in check, that he lived very well with her up to his death, leaving her to do as she pleased, and dying himself as fond as ever of the femme de chambre. A year before his death he had her married, but upon condition that the husband should not exercise his marital rights. He left her pregnant as well as his wife, both of whom lay-in after his decease. Madame de Berri, who was not jealous, retained this woman, and took care of her and her child.

The Duke abridged his life by his extreme intemperance in eating and drinking. He had concealed, besides, that in falling from his horse he had burst a blood-vessel. He threatened to dismiss any of his servants who should say that he had lost blood. A number of plates were found in the ruelle of his bed after his death. When he disclosed the accident it was too late to remedy it. As far as could be judged his illness proceeded from gluttony, in consequence of which emetics were so frequently administered to him that they hastened his death.

He himself said to his confessor, the Pere de la Rue, "Ah, father, I am myself the cause of my death!"

He repented of it, but not until too late.

SECTION XIX.—THE DUCHESSE DE BERRI.

My son loves his eldest daughter better than all the rest of his children, because he has had the care of her since she was seven years old. She was at that time seized with an illness which the physicians did not know how to cure. My son resolved to treat her in his own way. He succeeded in restoring her to health, and from that moment his love seemed to increase with her years. She was very badly educated, having been always left with femmes de chambre. She is not very capricious, but she is haughty and absolute in all her wishes.

> [Her pride led her into all sorts of follies. She once went through Paris preceded by trumpets and drama; and on another occasion she appeared at the theatre under a canopy. She received the Venetian Ambassador sitting in a chair elevated upon a sort of a platform. This haughtiness, however, did not prevent her from keeping very bad company, and she would sometimes lay aside her singularities and break up her orgies to pass some holy days at the Carmelites.]

From the age of eight years she has had entirely her own way, so that it is not surprising she should be like a headstrong horse. If she had been well brought up, she would have been a worthy character, for she has very good sense and a good natural disposition, and is not at all like her mother, to whom, although she was very severely treated, she always did her duty. During her mother's last illness, she watched her like a hired nurse. If Madame de Berri had been surrounded by honest people, who thought more of her honour than of their own interest, she would have been a very admirable person. She had excellent feelings; but as that old woman (Maintenon) once said, "bad company spoils good manners." To be pleasing she had only to speak, for she possessed natural eloquence, and could express herself very well.

Her complexion is very florid, for which she often lets blood, but without effect; she uses a great quantity of paint, I believe for the purpose of hiding the marks of the small-pox. She cannot dance, and hates it; but she is well-grounded in music. Her voice is neither strong nor agreeable, and yet she sings very correctly. She takes as much diversion as possible; one day she hunts, another day she goes out in a carriage, on a third she will go to a fair; at other times she frequents the rope-dancers, the plays, and the operas, and she goes everywhere 'en echarpe', and without stays. I often rally her, and say that she fancies she is fond of the chase, but in fact she only likes changing her place. She cares little about the result of the chase, but she likes boar-hunting better than stag-hunting, because the former furnishes her table with black puddings and boars' heads.

I do not reckon the Duchesse de Berri among my grandchildren. She is separated from me, we live like strangers to each other, she does not disturb herself about me, nor I about her. (7th January, 1716.)

Madame de Maintenon was so dreadfully afraid lest the King should take a fancy to the Duchesse de Berri while the Dauphine was expected, that she did her all sorts of ill offices. After the Dauphine's death she repaired the wrong; but then, to tell the truth, the King's inclination was not so strong.

If the Duchesse de Berri was not my daughter-in-law, I should have no reason to be dissatisfied with her; she behaves politely to me, which is all that I can say. (25th Sept., 1716.)

She often laughs at her own figure and shape. She has certainly good sense, and is not very punctilious. Her flesh is firm and healthy, her cheeks are as hard as stone. I should be ungrateful not to love her, for she does all sorts of civil things towards me, and displays so great a regard for me that I am often quite amazed at it. (12th April, 1718.)

She is magnificent in her expenditure; to be sure she can afford to be so, for her income amounts to 600,000 livres. Amboise was her jointure, but she preferred Meudon.

She fell sick on the 28th March, 1719. I went to see her last Sunday, the 23rd May, and found her in a sad state, suffering from pains in her toes and the soles of her feet until the tears came into her eyes. I went away because I saw that she refrained from crying out on my account. I thought she was in a bad way. A consultation was held by her three physicians, the result of which was that they determined to bleed her in the feet. They had some difficulty in persuading her to submit to it, because the pain in her feet was so great that she uttered the most piercing screams if the bedclothes only rubbed against them. The bleeding, however, succeeded, and she was in some degree relieved. It was the gout in both feet.

The feet are now covered with swellings filled with water, which cause her as much pain as if they were ulcers; she suffers day and night. Whatever they may say, there has been no other swelling of the feet since those blisters appeared. (13th June.)

The swelling has now entirely disappeared, but the pain is greater than before. All the toes are covered with transparent blisters; she cries out so that she may be heard three rooms off. The doctors now confess they do not know what the disorder is. (20th June.) The King's surgeon says it is rheumatic gout. (11th July.) I believe that frequent and excessive bathing and gluttony have undermined her health. She has two fits of fever daily, and the disease does not abate. She is not impatient nor peevish; the emetic given to her the day before yesterday causes her much pain; it seems that from time to time rheumatic pains have affected her shoulders without her taking much notice of them. From being very fat, as she was, she has become thin and meagre. Yesterday she confessed, and received the communion. (18th July.) She was bled thrice before she took the emetic. (Tuesday, 18th July.) She received the last Sacrament with a firmness which deeply affected her attendants. Between two and three o'clock this night (19th July) she died. Her end was a very easy one; they say she died as if she had gone to sleep. My son remained with her until she lost all consciousness, which was about an hour before her death. She was his favourite daughter. The poor Duchesse de Berri was as much the cause of her own death as if she had blown her brains out, for she secretly ate melons, figs and milk; she herself confessed, and her doctor told me, that she had closed her room to him and to the other medical attendants for a fortnight that she might indulge in this way. Immediately after the storm she began to die. Yesterday evening she said to me: "Oh, Madame! that clap of thunder has done me great harm;" and it was evident that it had made her worse.

My son has not been able to sleep. The poor Duchesse de Berri could not have been saved; her brain was filled with water; she had an ulcer in the stomach and another in the groin; her liver was affected, and her spleen full of disease. She was taken by night to St. Denis, whither all her household accompanied her corse. They were so much embarrassed about her funeral oration that it was resolved ultimately not to pronounce one.

With all her wealth she has left my son 400,000 livres of debt to pay. This poor Princess was horribly robbed and pillaged. You may imagine what a race these favourites are; Mouchi, who enjoyed the greatest favour, did not grieve for her mistress a single moment; she was playing the flute at her window on the very day that the Princess was borne to St. Denis, and went to a large dinner party in Paris, where she ate and drank as if nothing had happened, at the same time talking in so impertinent a manner as disgusted all the guests. My son desired her and her husband to quit Paris.

My son's affliction is so much the greater since he perceives that, if he had been less complying with his beloved daughter, and if he had exercised somewhat more of a parent's authority, she would have been alive and well at this time.

That Mouchi and her lover Riom have been playing fine tricks; they had duplicate keys, and left the poor Duchess without a sou. I cannot conceive what there is to love in this Riom; he has neither face nor figure; he looks, with his green-and-yellow complexion, like a water fiend; his mouth, nose and eyes are like those of a Chinese. He is more like a baboon than a Gascon, which he is. He is a very dull person, without the least pretensions to wit; he has a large head, which is sunk between a pair of very broad shoulders, and his appearance is that of a low-minded person; in short, he is a very ugly rogue.

And yet the toad does not come of bad blood; he is related to some of the best families. The Duc de Lauzun is his uncle, and Biron his nephew. He is, nevertheless, unworthy of the honour which was conferred on him; for he was only a captain in the King's Guard. The women all ran after him; but, for my part, I find him extremely disagreeable; he has an unhealthy air and looks like one of the Indian figures upon a screen.

He was not here when Madame de Berri died, but was with the army, in the regiment which had been bought for him. When the news of the Duchess's death reached him the Prince de Conti went to seek Riom, and sang a ridiculous song, my son was a little vexed at this, but he did not take any notice of it.

There can be no doubt that the Duchess was secretly married to Riom; this has consoled me in some degree for her loss. I had heard it said before, and I made a representation upon the subject to my granddaughter.

She laughed, and replied: "Ah, Madame, I thought I had the honour of being so well known to you that you could not believe me guilty of so great a folly; I who am so much blamed for my pride."

This answer lulled my suspicions, and I no longer believed the story. The father and mother would never have consented to this marriage; and even if they had sanctioned such an impertinence I never would!

> [The Duchess, with her usual violence, teased her father to have her marriage made public; this was also Riom's most ardent desire, who had married her solely from ambitious motives. The Regent had despatched Riom to the army for the purpose of gaining time. One daughter was the result of the connection between Riom and the Duchesse de Berri, who was afterwards sent into a convent at Pontoisse.]

The toad had made the Princess believe that he was a Prince of the House of Aragon, and that the King of Spain unjustly withheld from him his kingdom; but that if she would marry him he could sue for his claim through the treaties of peace. Mouchi used to talk about this to the Duchess from morning to night; and it was for this reason that she was so greatly in favour.

That Mouchi is the granddaughter of Monsieur's late surgeon. Her mother, La Forcade, had been appointed by my son the gouvernante of his daughter and son, and thus the young Forcade was brought up with the Duchesse de Berri, who married her to Monsieur Mouchi, Master of the Wardrobe to the Duke, and gave her a large marriage-portion. While the King lived the Princess could not visit her much; and it was not until after his death that she became the favourite, and was appointed by the Duchess second dame d'atour.

SECTION XX.—MADEMOISELLE D'ORLEANS, LOUISE-ADELAIDE DE CHARTRES.

Mademoiselle de Chartres, Madame d'Orleans' second daughter, is well made, and is the handsomest of my granddaughters. She has a fine skin, a superb complexion, very white teeth, good eyes, and a faultless shape, but she stammers a little; her hands are extremely delicate, the red and white are beautifully and naturally mingled in her skin. I never saw finer teeth; they are like a row of pearls; and her gums are no less beautiful. A Prince of Auhalt who is here is very much in love with her; but the good gentleman is ugly enough, so that there is no danger. She dances well, and sings better; reads music at sight, and understands the accompaniment perfectly; and she sings without any grimace. She persists in her project of becoming a nun; but I think she would be better in the world, and do all in my power to change her determination: it seems, however, to be a folly which there is no eradicating. Her tastes are all masculine; she loves dogs, horses, and riding; all day long she is playing with gunpowder, making fusees and other artificial fireworks. She has a pair of pistols, which she is incessantly firing; she fears nothing in the world, and likes nothing which women in general like; she cares little about her person, and for this reason I think she will make a good nun.

She does not become a nun through jealousy of her sister, but from the fear of being tormented by her mother and sister, whom she loves very much, and in this she is right. She and her sister are not fond of their mother's favourites, and cannot endure to flatter them. They have no very reverent notions, either, of their mother's brother, and this is the cause of dissensions. I never saw my granddaughter in better spirits than on Sunday last; she was with her sister, on horseback, laughing, and apparently in great glee. At eight o'clock in the evening her mother arrived; we played until supper; I thought we were afterwards going to play again, but Madame d'Orleans begged me to go into the cabinet with her and Mademoiselle d'Orleans; the child there fell on her knees, and begged my permission, and her mother's, to go to Chelles to perform her devotions. I said she might do that anywhere, that the place mattered not, but that all depended upon her own heart, and the preparation which she made. She, however, persisted in her desire to go to Chelles. I said to her mother:

"You must decide whether your daughter shall go to Chelles or not."

She replied, "We cannot hinder her performing her devotions."

> [In the Memoirs of the time it is said that Mademoiselle de Chartres, being at the Opera with her mother, exclaimed, while Caucherau was singing a very tender air, "Ah! my dear Caucherau!" and that her mother, thinking this rather too expressive, resolved to send her to a convent.]

So yesterday morning at seven o'clock she set off in a coach; she afterwards sent back the carriage, with a letter to her father, her mother, and myself, declaring that she will never more quit that accursed cloister. Her mother, who has a liking for convents, is not very deeply afflicted; she looks upon it as a great blessing to be a nun, but, for my part, I think it is one of the greatest misfortunes.

My son went yesterday to Chelles, and took with him the Cardinal de Noailles, to try for the last time to bring his daughter away from the convent. (20th July, 1718.)

My heart is full when I think that our poor Mademoiselle d'Orleans has made the profession of her vows. I said to her all I could, in the hope of diverting her from this diabolical project, but all has been useless. (23rd August, 1718.) I should not have restrained my tears if I had been present at the ceremony of her profession. My son dreaded it also. I cannot tell for what reason Mademoiselle d'Orleans resolved to become a nun. Mademoiselle de Valois wanted to do the same thing, but she could not prevail upon her mother. In the convent they assume the names of saints. My granddaughter has taken that of Sister Bathilde; she is of the Benedictine order.

Madame d'Orleans has long wished her daughter to take this step, and it was on her account that the former Abbess, Villars' sister, was prevailed upon to quit the convent. He is in the interest of the Duc du Maine. I do not see, however, that his sister has much to complain of, for they gave her a pension of 12,000 livres until the first abbey should become vacant. Madame d'Orleans is, however, vexed at the idea of Villars' sister being obliged to yield to my son's daughter, which is, nevertheless, as it should be.

Our Abbess is upon worse terms than ever with her mother. She complains that the latter never comes but to scold her. She does not envy her sister her marriage, for she finds herself very happy, and in this she displays great good sense.

SECTION XXI.—MADEMOISELLE DE VALOIS, CHARLOTTE-AGLAE, CONSORT OF THE PRINCE OF MODENA.

Mademoiselle de Valois is not, in my opinion, pretty, and yet occasionally she does not look ugly. She has something like charms, for her eyes, her colour and her skin are good. She has white teeth, a large, ill-looking nose, and one prominent tooth, which when she laughs has a bad effect. Her figure is drawn up, her head is sunk between her shoulders, and what, in my opinion, is the worst part of her appearance, is the ill grace with which she does everything. She walks like an old woman of eighty. If she were a person not very anxious to please, I should not be surprised at the negligence of her gait; but she likes to be thought pretty. She is fond of dress, and yet she does not understand that a good mien and graceful manners are the most becoming dress, and that where these are wanting all the ornaments in the world are good for nothing. She has a good deal of the Mortemart family in her, and is as much like the Duchess of Sforza, the sister of Montespan, as if she were her daughter; the falsehood of the Mortemarts displays itself in her eyes. Madame d'Orleans would be the most indolent woman in the world but for Madame de Valois, her daughter, who is worse than she. To me nothing is more disgusting than a young person so indolent. She cares little for me, or rather cannot bear me, and, for my part, I care as little for a person so educated.

She is not upon good terms with her mother, because she wanted to marry her to the Prince de Dombes, the Duc du Maine's eldest son. The mother says now reproachfully to her daughter that, if she had married her nephew, neither his father's nor his own misfortunes would have taken place. She cannot bear to have her daughter in her sight, and has begged me to keep her with me.

My son has agreed to give his daughter to the Prince of Modem, at which I very sincerely rejoice. On the day before yesterday (28th November, 1719) she came hither with her mother to tell me that the courier had arrived. Her eyes were swollen and red, and she looked very miserable. The Duchess of Hanover tells me that the intended husband fell in love with Mademoiselle de Valois at the mere sight of her portrait. I think her rather pretty than agreeable. Her hawk nose spoils all, in my opinion. Her legs are long, her body stout and short, and her gait shows that she has not learnt to dance; in fact, she never would learn. Still, if the interior was as good as the exterior, all might pass; but she has as much of the father as of the mother in her, and this it is that I dislike.

Our bride-elect is putting, as we say here, as good a face as she can upon a bad bargain; although her language is gay her eyes are swollen, and it is suspected that she has been weeping all night. The Grand Prior, who is also General of the Galleys, will escort his sister into Italy. The Grand Duchess of Tuscany says that she will not see Mademoiselle de Valois nor speak to her, knowing very well what Italy is, and believing that Mademoiselle de Valois will not be able to reconcile herself to it. She is afraid that if her niece should ever return to France they will say, "There is the second edition of the Grand Duchess;" and that for every folly she may commit towards her father-in-law and husband they will add, "Such are the instructions which her aunt, the Grand Duchess, has given her." For this reason she said she would not go to see her.

The present has come from Modena; it does not consist of many pieces; there is a large jewel for the bride, with some very fine diamonds, in the midst of which is the portrait of the Prince of Modena, but it is badly executed. This present is to be given on the day of the marriage and at the signature of the contract in the King's presence; this ceremony will take place on the 11th (of February, 1720). The nuptial benediction will be pronounced on Monday, and on Thursday she will set off. I never in my life saw a bride more sorrowful; for the last three days she has neither eaten nor drunk, and her eyes are filled with tears.

I have been the prophetess of evil, but I have prophesied too truly. When our Princess of Modena told me that she wished to go to Chelles to bid her sister farewell, I told her that the measles had been in the convent a short time before, that the Abbess herself had been attacked by this disease, which was contagious. She replied that she would seek it. I said such things are more easily found than anything good; you run a risk of your life, and I recommend you to take care. Notwithstanding my advice, she went on Sunday morning to Chelles, and passed the whole of the day with her sister. Soon afterwards she found herself unwell, and was laid up with the measles. Her consolation is that this illness retards her journey.

On the 12th of March (1720) my son brought his daughter to bid me farewell. She could not articulate a word. She took my hands, kissed and pressed them, and then clasped her own. My son was much affected when he brought her. They thought at first of marrying her to the Prince of Piedmont. Her father had given her some reason to hope for this union, but he afterwards retracted.

> [According to Duclos it was Madame herself who prevented this marriage by writing to the Queen of Sicily that she was too much her friend to make her so worthless a present as Mademoiselle de Valois. Duclos adds that the Regent only laughed at this German blunder of his mother's.]

She would have preferred marrying the Duke or the Comte de Charolois, because then she would have remained with her friends. Her father has given her several jewels. The King's present is superb. It consists of fourteen very large and fine diamonds, to each of which are fastened round pearls of the first water, and together they form a necklace. The Grand Duchess advised her niece well in telling her not to follow her example, but to endeavour to please her husband and father-in-law.

> [The same author (Duclos) says, on the contrary, that the Duchess had given her niece the following advice: "My dear, do as I have done. Have one or two children and try to get back to France; there is nothing good for us out of that country."]

The Prince of Modena will repair to Genoa incognito, because the Republic has declared that they will pay due honours to his bride as a Princess of the blood, but not as Princess of Modena. They have already begun to laugh here at the amusements of Modena. She has sent to her father from Lyons an harangue which was addressed to her by a curate. In spite of her father, she will visit the whole of

Provence. She will go to Toulon, La Ste. Beaume, and I know not what. I believe she wishes to see everything or anything except her husband.

> [She performed her journey so slowly that the Prince complained of it, and the Regent was obliged to order his daughter to go directly to the husband, who was expecting her.]

It may truly be said of this Princess that she has eaten her white bread first.

All goes well at Modena at present, but the too charming brother-in-law is not permitted to be at the petite soupers of his sister. The husband, it is said, is delighted with his wife; but she has told him that he must not be too fond of her, for that is not the fashion in France, and would seem ridiculous. This declaration has not, as might be guessed, given very great satisfaction in this country.

The Grand Duchess says, in the time of the Queen-mother's regency, when the Prince and his brother, the Prince de Conti, were taken to the Bastille, they were asked what books they would have to amuse themselves with? The Prince de Conti said he should like to have "The Imitation of Jesus Christ;" and the Prince de Condo said he would rather like "The Imitation of the Duc de Beaufort," who had then just left the Bastille.

"I think," added the Duchess, "that the Princess of Modena will soon be inclined to ask for 'The Imitation of the Grand Duchess.'"

[The Princess of Modena did, in fact, go back to France, and remained there for the rest of her life.]

Our Princess of Modena has found her husband handsomer and likes him better than she thought she should; she has even become so fond of him, that she has twice kissed his hands; a great condescension for a person so proud as she is, and who fancies that, there is not her equal on the earth.

The Duke of Modena is a very strange person in all matters. His son and his son's wife have requested him to get rid of Salvatico, who has been here in the quality of envoy. This silly person made on the journey a declaration in form of his love for the Princess, and threatened her with all sorts of misfortune if she did not accept his love. He began his declaration with,

"Ah! ah! ah! Madame, ah! ah! ah! Madame."

The Princess interrupted him: "What do you mean with your ah's?"

He replied, "Ah! the Prince of Modena is under great obligations; I have made him happy."

He had begun the same follies here, and was in the habit of entering the Princess's chamber at all times, and he even had the impudence to be jealous. The Princess complained of him to her husband, and he told his father of it, begging him to send the rogue away; but the father was so far from complying that he wanted to make Salvatico his major-domo. Upon the whole, I think that Salvatico's love for our Princess of Modena is fortunate for her; for, having learnt all that had passed here,

[Mademoiselle de Valois had an amorous intrigue with the Duc de
Richelieu; and it is said that she only consented to marry the
Prince of Modena upon condition that her father, the Regent, would
set her husband at liberty. Madame had intimated to the Duc de
Richelieu that, if he approached the places where her granddaughter
was with her, his life would be in great peril.]

he might have made inconvenient reports: he would, however, perhaps have done it in vain, for the Prince would not have believed him. Salvatico is quite crazy. He is the declared favourite of the Duke of Modena, which verifies the German proverb, "Like will to like, as the devil said to the collier."

The Prince and Princess are very fond of each other; but it is said they join in ridiculing the old father (2nd August, 1720). The Princess goes about all day from room to room, crying, "How tired I am, how tiresome everything is here!" She, however, lives a little better with her husband than at the beginning.

SECTION XXII.—THE ILLEGITIMATE CHIL-DREN OF THE REGENT, DUC D'ORLEANS.

My son has three illegitimate children, two boys and a girl; but only one of them is legitimated, that is, his son by Mademoiselle de Seri, a lady of noble family, and who was my Maid of Honour. The younger Margrave of Anspach was also in love with her. This son is called the Chevalier d'Orleans. The other, who is now (1716) about eighteen years old, is an Abbe; he is the son of La Florence, a dancer at the Opera House. The daughter is by Desmarets, the actress. My son says that the Chevalier d'Orleans is more unquestionably his than any of the others; but, to tell the truth, I think the Abbe has a stronger family likeness to my son than the Chevalier, who is like none of them. I do not know where my son found him; he is a good sort of person, but he has neither elegance nor beauty. It is a great pity that the Abbe is illegitimate: he is well made; his features are not bad; he has very good talents, and has studied much.—[Duclos says that this 'eleve' of the Jesuits was, nevertheless, the most zeal-ous ignoramus that ever their school produced.]—He is a good deal like the portraits of the late Monsieur in his youth, only that he is bigger. When he stands near Mademoiselle de Valois it is easy to see that they belong to the same father. My son purchased for the Chevalier d'Orleans the office of General of the Galleys from the Marechal de Tasse. He intends to make him a Knight of Malta, so that he may live unmarried, for my son does not wish to have the illegitimate branches of his family extended. The Chevalier does not want wit; but he is a little satirical, a habit which he takes from his mother.

My son will not recognize the Abbe Saint-Albin, on account of the irregular life which his mother, La Florence, has led. He fears being laughed at for acknowledging children so different. The Abbe Du-bois was a chief cause, too, why my son would not acknowledge this son. It was because the Abbe, aspiring to the Cardinal's hat, was jealous of every one who might be a competitor with him. I love this Abbe Saint-Albin, in the first place, because he is attached to me, and, in the second, because he is really very clever; he has wit and sense, with none of the mummery of priests. My son does not esteem him half so much as he deserves, for he is one of the best persons in the world; he is pious and virtuous, learned in every point, and not vain. It is in vain for my son to deny him; any one may see of what race he comes, and I am sorry that he is not legitimated. My son is much more fond of Seri's Son.

The poor Abbe de Saint-Albin is grieved to death at not being acknowledged; while Fortune smiles upon his elder brother, he is forgotten, despised, and has no rank; he seeks only to be legitimated. I console him as well as I can; but why should I tease my son about the business?

[The Abbe de Saint-Albin was appointed Bishop of Laon, and, after

Dubois' death, Archbishop of Cambrai. When he wished to become a

member of the Parliament he could not give the names either of his

father or mother; he had been baptized in the name of Cauche, the

Regent's valet de chambre and purveyor.]

It would only put him in the way of greater inconveniences, for, as he has also several children by Parabere, she would be no less desirous that he should legitimate hers. This consideration ties my tongue.

The daughter of the actress Desmarets is somewhat like her mother, but she is like no one else. She was educated in a convent at Saint Denis, but had no liking for a nun's life. When my son had her first brought to him she did not know who she was. When my son told her he was her father, she was transported with joy, fancying that she was the daughter of Seri and sister to the Chevalier; she thought, too, that she would be legitimated immediately. When my son told her that could not be done, and that she was Desmarets' daughter, she wept excessively. Her mother had never been permitted to see her in the convent; the nuns would not have allowed it, and her presence would have been injurious to the child. From the time she was born, her mother had not seen her until the present year (1719), when she saw her in a box at the theatre, and wept for joy. My son married this girl to the Marquis de Segur.

An actress at the Opera House, called Mdlle. d'Usg, who is since dead, was in great favour with my son, but that did not last long. At her death it appeared that, although she had had several children, neither she nor her mother nor her grandmother had ever been married.

SECTION XXIII.—THE CHEVALIER DE LOR-RAINE.

The Chevalier de Lorraine looked very ill, but it was in conse-quence of his excessive debauchery, for he had once been a hand-some man. He had a well-made person, and if the interior had an-swered to the exterior I should have had nothing to say against him. He was, however, a very bad man, and his friends were no better than he. Three or four years before my husband's death, and for his satisfaction, I was reconciled with the Chevalier, and from that time he did me no mischief. He was always before so much afraid of being sent away that he used to tell Monsieur he ought to know what I was saying and doing, that he might be apprised of any at-tempt that should be made against the Chevalier or his creatures.

He died so poor that his friends were obliged to bury him; yet he had 100,000 crowns of revenue, but he was so bad a manager that his people always robbed him. Provided they would supply him when he wanted them with a thousand pistoles for his pleasures or his play, he let them dispose of his property as they thought fit. That Grancey drew large sums from him. He met with a shocking death. He was standing near Madame de Mare, Grancey's sister, and tell-ing her that he had been sitting up at some of his extravagant pleas-ures all night, and was uttering the most horrible expressions, when suddenly he was stricken with apoplexy, lost the power of speech, and shortly afterwards expired.

> [He died suddenly in his own house, playing at ombre, as many of his family had done, and was regretted by no person except Mdlle. de Lil-lebonne, to whom he was believed to have been privately married.
>
> —Note to Dangeau's Journal. This man, who was suspected of having poisoned the King's sis-ter-in-law, was nevertheless in possession of four

abbeys, the revenues of which defrayed the expenses of his debaucheries.]

SECTION XXIV.—PHILIP V., KING OF SPAIN.

Louis XIV. wept much when his grandson set out for Spain. I could not help weeping, too. The King accompanied him as far as Sceaux. The tears and lamentations in the drawing-room were irresistible. The Dauphin was also deeply affected.

The King of Spain is very hunchbacked, and is not in other respects well made; but he is bigger than his brothers. He has the best mien, good features, and fine hair. What is somewhat singular, although his hair is very light, his eyes are quite black; his complexion is clear red and white; he has an Austrian mouth; his voice is deep, and he is singularly slow in speaking. He is a good and peaceable sort of a person, but a little obstinate when he takes it in his head. He loves his wife above all things, leaves all affairs to her, and never interferes in anything. He is very pious, and believes he should be damned if he committed any matrimonial infidelity. But for his devotion he would be a libertine, for he is addicted to women, and it is for this reason he is so fond of his wife. He has a very humble opinion of his own merit. He is very easily led, and for this reason the Queen will not lose sight of him. He receives as current truths whatever is told him by persons to whom he is accustomed, and never thinks of doubting. The good gentleman ought to be surrounded by competent persons, for his own wit would not carry him far; but he is of a good disposition, and is one of the quietest men in the world. He is a little melancholy, and there is nothing in Spain to make him gay.

He must know people before he will speak to them at all. If you desire him to talk you must tease him and rally him a little, or he will not open his mouth. I have seen Monsieur very impatient at his talking to me while he could not get a word from him. Monsieur did not take the trouble to talk to him before he was a King, and then he wished him to speak afterwards; that did not suit the King. He was not the same with me. In the apartment, at table, or at the play, he used to sit beside me. He was very fond of hearing tales, and I used to tell them to him for whole evenings: this made him well accustomed to me, and he had always something to ask me. I have often laughed at the answer he made me when I said to him, "Come, Monsieur, why do not you talk to your uncle, who is quite distressed that you never speak to him."

"What shall I say to him?" he replied, "I scarcely know him."

It is quite true that the Queen of Spain was at first very fond of the Princesse des Ursins, and that she grieved much when that Princess was dismissed for the first time. The story that is told of the Confessor is also very true; only one circumstance is wanting in it, that is, that the Duc de Grammont, then Ambassador, played the part of the Confessor, and it was for this reason he was recalled.

The Queen had one certain means of making the King do whatever she wished. The good gentleman was exceedingly fond of her, and this fondness she turned to good account. She had a small truckle-bed in her room, and when the King would not comply with any of her requests she used to make him sleep in this bed; but when she was pleased with him he was admitted to her own bed; which was the very summit of happiness to the poor King. After the Princesse des Ursins had departed, the King recalled the Confessor from Rome, and kept him near his own person (1718).

The King of Spain can never forgive, and Madame des Ursins has told him so many lies to my son's disadvantage that the King can never, while he lives, be reconciled to him.

Rebenac's—[Francois de Feuquieres, Called the Comte de Rebenac, Extraordinary Ambassador to Spain.]—passion for the late Queen of Spain was of no disadvantage to her; she only laughed at it, and did not care for him. It was the Comte de Mansfeld, the man with the pointed nose, who poisoned her. He bought over two of her French femmes de chambre to give her poison in raw oysters; and they afterwards withheld from her the antidote which had been entrusted to their care.

The Queen of Spain, daughter of the first Madame,—[Henrietta of England.]—died in precisely the same manner as she did, and at the same age, but in a much more painful manner, for the violence of the poison was such as to make her nails fall off.

SECTION XXV.—THE DUCHESSE LOUISE-FRANCISQUE, CONSORT OF LOUIS III., DUC DE BOURBON.

I knew a German gentleman who has now been dead a long time (1718), who has sworn to me positively that the Duchess is not the daughter of the King, but of Marechal de Noailles. He noted the time at which he saw the Marshal go into Montespan's apartment, and it was precisely nine months from that time that the Duchess came into the world. This German, whose name was Bettendorf, was a brigadier in the Body Guard; and he was on guard at Montespan's when the captain of the first company paid this visit to the King's mistress.

The Duchess is not prettier than her daughters, but she has more grace; her manners are more fascinating and agreeable; her wit shines in her eyes, but there is some malignity in them also. I always say she is like a very pretty cat, which, while you play with it, lets you feel it has claws. No person has a better carriage of the head. It is impossible to dance better than the Duchess and her daughters can; but the mother dances the best. I do not know how it is, but even her lameness is becoming to her. The Duchess has the talent of saying things in so pleasant a manner that one cannot help laughing. She is very amusing and uncommonly good company; her notions are so very comical. When she wishes to make herself agreeable to any one she is very insinuating, and can take all shapes; if she were not also treacherous, one might say truly that nobody is more amiable than the Duchess; she understands so well how to accommodate herself to people's peculiar habits that one would believe she takes a real interest in them; but there is nothing certain about her. Although her sense is good, her heart is not. Notwithstanding her ambition, she seems at first as if she thought only of amusing and diverting herself and others; and she can feign so skilfully that one would think she had been very agreeably entertained in the society of persons, whom immediately upon her return home she will ridicule in all possible ways.

La Mailly complained to her aunt, old Maintenon, that her husband was in love with the Duchess; but this husband, having afterwards been captivated by an actress named Bancour, gave up to her all the Duchess's letters, for which he was an impertinent rascal. The Duchess wrote a song upon Mailly, in which she reproached her, notwithstanding her airs of prudery, with an infidelity with Villeroi, a sergeant of the Guard.

In the Duchess's house malice passes for wit, and therefore they are under no restraint. The three sisters — the Duchess, the Princesse de Conti, and Madame d'Orleans — behave to each other as if they were not sisters.

The Princess is a very virtuous person, and is much displeased at her daughter-in-law's manner of life, for Lasso is with her by day and by night; at the play, at the Opera, in visits, everywhere Lasso is seen with her.

SECTION XXVI. — THE YOUNGER DUCHESS.

The Duke's wife is not an ill-looking person: she has good eyes, and would be very well if she had not a habit of stretching and poking out her neck. Her shape is horrible; she is quite crooked; her back is curved into the form of an S. I observed her one day, through curiosity, when the Dauphine was helping her to dress.

She is a wicked devil; treacherous in every way, and of a very dangerous temper. Upon the whole, she is not good for much. Her falsehood was the means of preventing the Duke from marrying one of my granddaughters. Being the intimate friend of Madame de Berri, who was very desirous that one of her sisters should marry the Duke and the other the Prince de Conti, she promised to bring about the marriage, provided Madame de Berri would say nothing of it to the King or to me. After having imposed this condition, she told the King that Madame de Berri and my son were planning a marriage without his sanction; in order to punish them she begged the King to marry the Duke to herself, which was actually done.

Thanks to her good sense, she lives upon tolerable terms with her husband, although he has not much affection for her. They follow each their own inclinations; they are not at all jealous of each other, and it is said they have separate beds.

She causes a great many troubles and embarrassments to her relation, the young Princesse de Conti, and perfectly understands tormenting folks.

The young Duchess died yesterday evening (22nd March, 1720). The Duke's joy at the death of his wife will be greatly diminished when he learns that she has bequeathed to her sister, Mademoiselle de la Roche-sur-Yon, all her property; and as the husband and wife lived according to the custom of Paris, 'en communaute', the Duke will be obliged to refund the half of all he gained by Law's bank.

After the death of the younger Duchess, the Princesse de Conti, her mother, wrote to a Chevalier named Du Challar, who was the lover of the deceased, to beg him to come and see her, as he was the only object left connected with her daughter, and assuring him that he might reckon upon her services in everything that depended upon her. It was the younger Duchess who was so fond of Lasse, and who had been so familiar with him at a masked ball.

I recognized only two good qualities in her: her respect and affection for her grandmother, the Princess, and the skill with which she concealed her faults. Beside this, she was good for nothing, in whatever way her character is regarded. That she was treacherous is quite certain; and she shortened her life by her improper conduct. She neither loved nor hated her husband, and they lived together more like brother and sister than husband and wife.

The Elector of Bavaria, during his stay at Paris, instead of visiting his nephews and nieces, passed all his time, by day and by night, with the Duchess and her daughters. As to me, he fled me as he would fly the plague, and never spoke to me but in the company of M. de Torcy. The Duchess had three of the handsomest daughters in the world: the one called Mademoiselle de Clermont is extremely beautiful; but I think her sister, the Princesse de Conti, more amiable. The Duchess can drink very copiously without being affected; her daughters would fain imitate her, but they soon get tipsy, and cannot control themselves as their mother can.

SECTION XXVII.—LOUIS III., DUC DE BOUR-BON.

It is said that the Duke has solid parts; he does everything with a certain nobility; he has a good person, but the loss of that eye, which the Duc de Berri struck out, disfigures him much. He is certainly very politic, and this quality he has from his mother. He is polite and well-bred; his mind is not very comprehensive, and he has been badly instructed. They say he is unfit for business for three reasons: first, on account of his ignorance; secondly, for his want of application; and, thirdly, for his impatience. I can see that in examining him narrowly one would find many defects in him; but he has also many praiseworthy qualities, and he possesses many friends. He has a greatness and nobility of soul, and a good deportment.

The Prince is in love with Madame de Polignac; but she is fond of the Duke, who cannot yet forget Madame de Nesle, although she has dismissed him to make room for that great calf, the Prince of Soubise. The latter person is reported to have said, "Why does the Duke complain? Have I not consented to share Madame de Nesle's favours with him whenever he chooses?"

Such is the delicacy which prevails here in affairs of love.

The Duke is very passionate. When Madame de Nesle dismissed him he almost died of vexation; he looked as if he was about to give up the ghost, and for six months he did not know what to do.

The Marquis de Villequier, the Duc d'Aumont's son, one day visited the Marquise de Nesle. She took it into her head to ask him if he was very fond of his wife. Villequier replied, "I am not in love with her; I see her very little; our humours differ greatly. She is serious, and for my part I like pleasure and gaiety. I feel for her a friendship founded on esteem, for she is one of the most virtuous women in France."

Madame de Nesle, of whom no man could say so much, took this for an insult, and complained of it to the Duke, who promised to avenge her. Some days afterwards he invited young Villequier to dine with him at the Marquis de Nesle's; there were, besides Madame de Nesle, the Marquis de Gevres, Madame de Coligny, and others. During dinner the Duke began thus:

"A great many men fancy they are sure of the fidelity of their wives, but it is a mistake. I thought to protect myself from this common fate by marrying a monster, but it served me nought; for a villain named Du Challar, who was more ugly than I am, played me false. As to the Marquis de Gevres, as he will never marry * * * , he will be exempt; but you, Monsieur de Nesle, you are so and so." Nesle, who did not believe it, although it was very true, only laughed. Then addressing himself to Villequier, he said, "And you, Villequier, don't you think you are so?" He was silent. The Duke continued, "Yes, you are befooled by the Chevalier de Pesay."

Villequier blushed, but at last said, "I confess that up to this moment I had no reason to believe it; but since you put me into such good company I have no right to complain."

I do not think Madame de Nesle was well revenged.

I remember that the Duke, who was terribly ill-made, said one day to the late Monsieur, who was a straight, well-formed person, that a mask had taken him for Monsieur. The latter, somewhat mortified at such a mistake, replied, "I lay that, with all other wrongs done to me, at the foot of the Cross."

Ever since the Duchess espoused the party of her son against her brother and his nephews, the Duke has displayed a great fondness for his mother, about whom he never disturbed himself before.

Mdlle. de Polignac made the Duke believe she was very fond of him. He entertained great suspicions of her, and had her watched, and learnt that she was carrying on a secret intrigue with the Chevalier of Bavaria. He reproached her with it, and she denied the accusation. The Duke cautioned her not to think that she could deceive him. She protested that he had been imposed upon. As soon, however, as she had quitted him she went to the Chevalier's house; and the Duke, who had her dogged, knew whither she had gone. The next day he appointed her to visit him; she went directly to the bedroom, believing that his suspicions were entirely lulled. The

Duke then opened the door wide, so that she might be seen from the cabinet, which was full of men; and calling the Chevalier of Bavaria, he said to him: "Here, Sir Chevalier, come and see your mistress, who will now have no occasion to go so far to find you."

Although the Duke and the Prince de Conti are brothers-in-law in two ways, they cannot bear each other.

The Duke is at this moment (1718) very strongly attached to Madame de Prie. She has already received a good beating on his account from her husband, but this does not deter her. She is said to have a good deal of sense; she entirely governs the Duke, who is solely occupied with making her unfaithful to M. de Prie. She has consoled the Duke for his dismissal from Madame de Nesle; but it is said that she is unfaithful to him, and that she has two other lovers. One is the Prince of Carignan, and the other Lior, the King's first maitre d'hotel, which latter is the handsomest of the three.

It is impossible that the Duke can now inspire any woman with affection for him. He is tall, thin as a lath; his legs are like those of a crane; his body is bent and short, and he has no calves to his legs; his eyes are so red that it is impossible to distinguish the bad eye from the good one; his cheeks are hollow; his chin so long that one would not suppose it belonged to the face; his lips uncommonly large: in short, I hardly ever saw a man before so ugly. It is said that the inconstancy of his mistress, Madame de Prie, afflicts him profoundly.

> The Marchioness was extremely beautiful, and her whole person was very captivating. Possessing as many mental as personal charms, she concealed beneath an apparent simplicity the most dangerous treachery. Without the least conception of virtue, which, according to her ideas, was a word void of sense, she affected innocence in vice, was violent under an appearance of meekness, and libertine by constitution. She deceived her lover with perfect impunity, who would believe what she said even against the evidence of his own eyes. I could mention several instances of this, if they were not too indecent. It is, however, sufficient to

say that she had one day to persuade him that he
was the cause of a libertinism of which he was really the victim.—Memoires de Duclos, tome ii. It is
well known that, after the Duke assumed the Regency, upon the death of the Regent, the Mar-
chioness du Prie governed in his name; and that
she was exiled, and died two years afterwards of
ennui and vexation.

The Princess of Modena takes nothing by the death of the Duchess; the Duke has said that he never would have married that Princess, and that now he will not marry at all.

In order that Mademoiselle de la Roche-sur-Yon may enjoy the
millions that belong to her of right, in consequence of her sister's
death, it is necessary first for her to receive them; but the Duke, it is
reported, as the good Duc de Crequi used to say, "Holds back as
tight as the trigger of the Cognac cross-bow;" and in fact he has not
only refused to give up to his sister what she should take under her
sister's will, but he disputes her right to the bank-notes which she
had given to the Duchess to take care of for her, when she herself
was dangerously ill.

The Duke and his mother are said to have gained each two hun-
dred and fifty millions.

The Duke, who is looked upon as Law's very good friend, has
been ill-treated by the people, who have passed all kinds of insults
upon him, calling him even a dog. His brother, the Marquis de
Clermont, too, has fared little better; for they cried after him at the
Port Royal, "Go along, dog! you are not much better than your
brother." His tutor alighted for the purpose of haranguing the mob;
but they picked up some stones, and he soon found it expedient to
get into the carriage again, and make off with all speed.

SECTION XXVIII.—FRANCOIS-LOUIS, PRINCE DE CONTI.

The Prince de Conti, who died lately (in 1709), had good sense, courage, and so many agreeable qualities as to make himself generally beloved. But he had also some bad points in his character, for he was false, and loved no person but himself.

It is said that he caused his own death by taking stimulating medicines, which destroyed a constitution naturally feeble. There had been some talk of making him King of Poland.—[In 1696, after the death of John Sobiesky.]

SECTION XXIX.—THE GREAT PRINCESSE DE CONTI, DAUGHTER OF LA VALLIERE.

This is of all the King's illegitimate daughters the one he most loves. She is by far the most polite and well-bred, but she is now totally absorbed by devotion.

SECTION XXX. — THE PRINCESS PALATINE, MARIE-THERESE DE BOURBON, WIFE OF FRANCOIS-LOUIS, PRINCE DE CONTI.

This Princess is the only one of the House of Conde who is good for anything. I think she must have some German blood in her veins. She is little, and somewhat on one side, but she is not hunchbacked. She has fine eyes, like her father; with this exception, she has no pretensions to beauty, but she is virtuous and pious. What she has suffered on account of her husband has excited general compassion; he was as jealous as a fiend, though without the slightest cause. She never knew where she was to pass the night. When she had made arrangements to sleep at Versailles, he would take her from Paris to Chantilly, where she supposed she was going to stay; then she was obliged to set out for Versailles. He tormented her incessantly in all possible ways, and he looked, moreover, like a little ape. The late Queen had two paroquets, one of which was the very picture of the Prince, while the other was as much like the Marechal de Luxembourg as one drop of water is like another.

Notwithstanding all that the Princess has suffered, she daily regrets the loss of her husband. I am often quite angry to see her bewailing her widowhood instead of enjoying the repose which it affords her; she wishes that her husband were alive again, even although he should torment her again as much as before.

She was desirous that Mademoiselle de Conde should marry the late Margrave; this lady was incomparably more handsome than her sister; but I think he had a greater inclination for Mademoiselle de Vendome, because she seemed to be more modest and quiet.

The Princess, who has been born and educated here, had not the same dislike that I felt to her son's marrying an illegitimate child, and yet she has repented it no less. She is exceedingly unhappy with respect to her children. The Princesse de Conti, mother of the Prince de Conti, who is rather virtuous than otherwise, is nevertheless a little simpleton, and is something like the Comtesse Pimbeche

Orbeche, for she is always wishing to be engaged in lawsuits against her mother; who, on her part, has used all possible means, but without success, to be reconciled to her. On Thursday last (10th March, 1720) she lost her cause, and I am very glad of it, for it was an unjust suit. The younger Princess wished the affair to be referred to arbitration; but the son would have the business carried through, and made his counsel accuse his mother of falsehood. The advocate of the Princess replied as follows:

"The sincerity of the Princesse de Conti and of the Princess her daughter are so well known that all the world can judge of them." This has amused the whole palace.

SECTION XXXI.—LOUISE-ELIZABETH, PRINCESSE DE CONTI, CONSORT OF LOUIE- ARMAND DE CONTI.

[Illustration: Princesse de Conti—276]

She is a person full of charms, and a striking proof that grace is preferable to beauty. When she chooses to make herself agreeable, it is impossible to resist her. Her manners are most fascinating; she is full of gentleness, never displaying the least ill-humour, and always saying something kind and obliging. It is greatly to be regretted that she is not in the society of more virtuous persons, for she is herself naturally very good; but she is spoiled by bad company. She has an ugly fool for her husband, who has been badly brought up; and the examples which are constantly before her eyes are so pernicious that they have corrupted her and made her careless of her reputation. Her amiable, unaffected manners are highly delightful to foreigners. Among others, some Bavarians have fallen in love with her, as well as the Prince Ragotzky; but she disgusted him with her coquetry.

She does not love her husband, and cannot do so, no less on account of his ugly person than for his bad temper. It is not only his face that is hideous, but his whole person is frightful and deformed. She terrified him by placing some muskets and swords near her bed, and assuring him that if he came there again with his pistols charged, she would take the gun and fire upon him, and if she missed, she would fall upon him with the sword. Since this time he has left off carrying his pistols.

Her husband teased her, and made her weep so much that she has lost her child, and her health is again injured.

SECTION XXXII. — LOUIE-ARMAND, PRINCE DE CONTI.

It cannot be denied that his whole appearance is extremely repulsive. He is a horribly ill-made little man, and is always absent-minded, which gives him a distracted air, as if he were really crazy. When it could be the least expected, too, he will fall over his own walking-stick. The folks in the palace were so much accustomed to this in the late King's time, that they used always to say, when they heard anything fall,

"It's nothing; only the Prince de Conti tumbling down."

He has sense, but he has been brought up like a scullion boy; he has strange whimsies, of which he is quite aware himself, but which he cannot control. His wife is a charming woman, and is much to be pitied for being in fear of her life from this madman, who often threatens her with loaded pistols. Fortunately, she has plenty of courage and does not fear him. Notwithstanding this, he is very fond of her; and this is the more surprising, because his love for the sex is not very strong; and although he visits improper places occasionally, it is only for the purpose of tormenting the poor wretches who are to be found there. Before he was married he felt no, affection for any woman but his mother, who also loved him very tenderly. She is now vexed at having no longer the same ascendency over her son, and is jealous of her daughter-in-law because the Prince loves her alone. This occasions frequent disturbances in the house. The mother has had a house: built at some distance from her son. When they are good friends, she dismisses the workmen; but when they quarrel, she doubles the number and hastens the work, so that one may always tell, upon a mere inspection of the building, upon what terms the Princesse de Conti and her son are living. The mother wished to have her grandson to educate; her daughter-in-law opposed it because she preferred taking care of him herself; and then ensued a dog-and-cat quarrel. The wife, who is cunning enough, governs her husband entirely, and has gained over his favourites to be her creatures. She is the idol of the-whole house.

In order to prevent the Prince de Conti from going to Hungary, the government of Poitou has been bought for him, and a place in the Council of the Regency allotted to him; by this means they have retained the wild beast.

Our young Princess says her husband has a rheum in his eyes.

To amuse her, he reads aloud Ovid in the original; and although she does not understand one word of Latin, she is obliged to listen and to remain silent, even though any one should come in; for if anybody interrupts him he is angry, and scolds all who are in the apartment.

At the last masked ball (4th March, 1718) some one who had dressed himself like the Prince de Conti, and wore a hump on his back, went and sat beside him. "Who are you, mask?" asked the Prince.

The other replied, "I am the Prince de Conti."

Without the least ill-temper, the Prince took off his mask, and, laughing, said, "See how a man may be deceived. I have been fancying for the last twenty years that I was the Prince de Conti." To keep one's temper on such an occasion is really an uncommon thing.

The Prince thought himself quite cured, but he has had a relapse in Spain, and, although he is a general of cavalry, he cannot mount his horse. I said on Tuesday last (17th July, 1719) to the young Princesse de Conti that I heard her husband was not entirely recovered. She laughed and whispered to me,—

"Oh, yes, he is quite well; but he pretends not to be so that he may avoid going to the siege, where he may be killed, for he is as cowardly as an ape." I think if I had as little inclination for war as he has, I would not engage in the campaign at all; there is nothing to oblige him to do so-it is to reap glory, not to encounter shame, that men go into the army. His best friends, Lanoue and Cleremont, for example, have remonstrated with him on this subject, and he has quarrelled with them in consequence. It is an unfortunate thing for a man not to know himself.

The Prince is terribly afflicted with a dysentery. They wanted to carry him to Bayonne, but he has so violent a fever that he would not be able to support the journey. He is therefore obliged to stay with the army (25th August, 1719).

He has been back nine or ten days, but I have heard nothing of him yet; he is constantly engaged in the Rue de Quincampoix, trying to gain money among the stock-jobbers (19th September, 1719).

At length he has been to see me. Perhaps there was this morning less stock-jobbing than usual in the Rue de Quincampoix, for there he has been ever since his return. His cousin, the Duke, is engaged in the same pursuit. The Prince de Conti has not brought back much honour from the campaign; he is too much addicted to debauchery of all kinds.

Although he can be polite when he chooses, no one can behave more brutally than he does occasionally, and he becomes more and more mad daily.

At one of the last opera balls he seized a poor little girl just come from the country, took her from her mother's side, and, placing her between his own legs, amused himself by slapping and filliping her until he made her nose and mouth bleed. The young girl, who had done nothing to offend him, and who did not even know him, wept bitterly; but he only laughed, and said, "Cannot I give nice fillips?" All who were witnesses of this brutal scene pitied her; but no one dared come to the poor child's assistance, for they were afraid of having anything to do with this violent madman. He makes the most frightful grimaces, and I, who am extremely frightened at crazy people, tremble whenever I happen to be alone with him.

His wicked pranks remind me of my own. When I was a child I used to take touchwood, and, placing pieces of it over my eyes and in my mouth, I hid myself upon the staircase for the purpose of terrifying the people; but I was then much afraid of ghosts, so that I was always the first to be frightened. It is in the same way that the Prince de Conti does; he wishes to make himself feared, and he is the most timid person in the world.

The Duke and his mother, as well as Lasse, the friend of the latter, have gained several millions. The Prince has gained less, and yet his winnings, they say, amount to millions.

> [He had four wagons loaded with silver carried from Law's bank, in exchange for his paper money; and this it was that accelerated Law's disgrace, and created a kind of popularity for the Prince de Conti.]

The two cousins do not stir from the Rue de Quincampoix, which has given rise to the following epigram:

> Prince dites nous vos exploits
> Que faites vous pour votre gloire?
> Taisez-vous sots! — Lisez l'histoire
> De la rue de Quincampoix.

But the person who had gained most by this affair is Dantin, who is horridly avaricious.

The Princesse de Conti told me that she had had her son examined in his infancy by Clement, for the purpose of ascertaining whether he was in every respect well made; and that he, having found the child perfectly well made, went to the Prince de Conti, and said to him: "Monseigneur, I have examined the shape of the young Prince who is just born: he is at all points well formed, let him sleep without a bolster that he may remain so; and only imagine what grief it would occasion to the Princesse de Conti, who has brought him into the world straight, if you should make him crooked."

The Prince de Conti wished to speak of something else, but Clement still returned to the same topic, saying, "Remember, Monseigneur, he is straight as a wand, and do not make him crooked and hunchbacked."

The Prince de Conti, not being able to endure this, ran away.

SECTION XXXIII.—THE ABBE DUBOIS.

My son had a sub-governor, and he it was who appointed the Abbe, a very learned person, to be his tutor. The sub-governor's intention was to have dismissed the Abbe as soon as he should have taught my son sufficiently, and, excepting during the time occupied by the lessons, he never suffered him to remain with his pupil. But this good gentleman could not accomplish his design; for being seized with a violent colic, he died, unhappily for me, in a few hours. The Abbe then proposed himself to supply his place. There was no other preceptor near at hand, so the Abbe remained with my son, and assumed so adroitly the language of an honest man that I took him for one until my son's marriage; then it was that I discovered all his knavery. I had a strong regard for him, because I thought he was tenderly attached to my son, and only desired to promote his advantage; but when I found that he was a treacherous person, who thought only of his own interest, and that, instead of carefully trying to preserve my son's honour, he plunged him into ruin by permitting him to give himself up to debauchery without seeming to perceive it, then my esteem for this artful priest was changed into disgust. I know, from my son himself, that the Abbe, having one day met him in the street, just as he was about to enter a house of ill-fame, did nothing but laugh at him, instead of taking him by the arm and leading him home again. By this culpable indulgence, and by the part he took in my son's marriage, he has proved that there is neither faith nor honesty in him. I know that I do him no wrong in suspecting him to have contributed to my son's marriage; what I say I have from my son himself, and from people who were living with that old Maintenon at the time, when the Abbe used to go nightly for the purpose of arranging that intrigue with her, the object of which was to sell and betray his master. He deceives himself if he fancies that I do not know all this. At first he had declared in my favour, but after the old woman had sent for him two or three times he suddenly changed his conduct. It was not, however, on this that the King afterwards took a dislike to him, but for a nefarious scheme in which he was engaged with the Pere La Chaise. Monsieur was as much vexed as I. The King and the old woman threatened to dismiss all his favourites, which made him consent to everything; he repented afterwards, but it was then too late.

I would to God that the Abbe Dubois had as much religion as he has talent! but he believes in nothing—he is treacherous and wicked—his falsehood may be seen in his very eyes. He has the look of a fox; and his device is an animal of this sort, creeping out of his hole and watching a fowl. He is unquestionably a good scholar, talks well, and has instructed my son well; but I wish he had ceased to visit his pupil after his tuition was terminated. I should not then have to regret this unfortunate marriage, to which I can never reconcile myself. Excepting the Abbe Dubois there is no priest in my son's favour. He has a sort of indistinctness in his speech, which makes it sometimes necessary for him to repeat his words; and this often annoys me.

If there is anything which detracts from the Abbe's good sense it is his extreme pride; it is a weak side upon which he may always be successfully attacked. I wish my son had as little confidence in him as I have; but what astonishes me most is that, knowing him as he does, better than I do, he will still trust him. My son is like the rest of his family; he cannot get rid of persons to whom he is accustomed, and as the Abbe has been his tutor, he has acquired a habit of suffering him to say anything he chooses. By his amusing wit, too, he always contrives to restore himself to my son's good graces, even when the latter has been displeased with him.

If the Abbe had been choked with his first lie he had been dead long ago. Lying is an art in which he excels, and the more eminently where his own interest is concerned; if I were to enumerate all the lies I have known him to utter I should have a long list to write. He it was who suggested to the King all that was necessary to be said to him respecting my son's marriage, and for this purpose he had secret interviews with Madame de Maintenon. He affects to think we are upon good terms, and whatever I say to him, however disagreeable, he takes it all with a smile.

My son has most amply recompensed the Abbe Dubois; he has given him the place of Secretary of the King's Cabinet, which M. Calieres formerly held, and which is worth 22,000 livres; he has also given him a seat in the Council of Regency for the Foreign Affairs.

My son assures me that it is not his intention to make the Abbe Dubois a Cardinal, and that the Abbe himself does not think about it (17th August, 1717).

On the 6th of March, this disagreeable priest came to me and said, "Monseigneur has just nominated me Archbishop of Cambrai." I replied, "I congratulate you upon it; but has this taken place today? I heard of it a week ago; and, since you were seen to take the oaths on your appointment, no one has doubted it." It is said that the Duc de Mazarin said, on the Abbe's first Mass, "The Abbe Dubois is gone to his first communion;" meaning that he had never before taken the communion in all his life. I embarrassed my son by remarking to him that he had changed his opinion since he told me the Abbe should never become Bishop or Archbishop, and that he did not think of being Cardinal. My son blushed and answered, "It is very true; but I had good reason for changing my intention." "Heaven grant it may be so," I said, "for it must be by God's mercy, and not from the exercise of your own reason."

The Archbishop of Cambrai is the declared enemy of our Abbe Saint-Albin. The word arch is applicable to all his qualities; he is an arch-cheat, an arch-hypocrite, an arch-flatterer, and, above all, an arch-knave.

It is reported that a servant of the Archbishop of Rheims said to a servant of the Archbishop of Cambrai, "Although my master is not a Cardinal, he is still a greater lord than yours, for he consecrates the Kings."

"Yes," replied the Abbe Dubois' servant, "but my master consecrates the real God, who is still greater than all Kings."

SECTION XXXIV.—MR. LAW.

Mr. Law is a very honest and a very sensible man; he is extremely polite to everybody, and very well bred. He does not speak French ill—at least, he speaks it much better than Englishmen in general. It is said that when his brother arrived in Paris, Mr. Law made him a present of three millions (of livres); he has good talents, and has put the affairs of the State in such good order that all the King's debts have been paid. He is admirably skilled in all that relates to finance. The late King would have been glad to employ him, but, as Mr. Law was not a Catholic, he said he ought not to confide in him (19th Sept., 1719).

He (Law) says that, of all the persons to whom he has explained his system, there have been only two who have properly comprehended it, and these are the King of Sicily and my son; he was quite astonished at their having so readily understood it. He is so much run after, that he has no repose by day or by night. A Duchess even kissed his hand publicly.

If a Duchess can do this, what will not other ladies do?

Another lady, who pursued him everywhere, heard that he was at Madame de Simiane's, and immediately begged the latter to permit her to dine with her. Madame de Simiane went to her and said she must be excused for that day, as Mr. Law was to dine with her. Madame de Bouchu replied that it was for this reason expressly she wished to be invited. Madame de Simiane only repeated that she did not choose to have Mr. Law troubled, and so quitted her. Having, however, ascertained the dinner-hour, Madame de Bouchu passed before the house in her coach, and made her coachman and footman call out "Fire!" Immediately all the company quitted the table to know where the fire was, and among them Mr. Law appeared. As soon as Madame de Bouchu saw him, she jumped out of her carriage to speak to him; but he, guessing the trick, instantly disappeared.

Another lady ordered her carriage to be driven opposite to Mr. Law's hotel and then to be overturned. Addressing herself to the coachman, she said, "Overturn here, you blockhead — overturn!" Mr. Law ran out to her assistance, when she confessed to him that she had done this for the sole purpose of having an interview with him.

[Illustration: Overturn here, you blockhead — 290]

A servant had gained so much in the Rue de Quincampoix, that he was enabled to set up his equipage. When his coach was brought home, he forgot who he was, and mounted behind. His servant cried out, "Ah, sir! what are you doing? this is your own carriage."

"That is true," said the quondam servant; "I had forgotten."

Mr. Law's coachman having also made a very considerable sum, demanded permission to retire from his service. His master gave it him, on condition of his procuring him another good coachman. On the next day, the wealthy coachman made his appearance with two persons, both of whom were, he said, good coachmen; and that Mr. Law had only to choose which of them he liked, while he, the coachman, would take the other.

People of all nations in Europe are daily coming to Paris; and it has been remarked that the number of souls in the capital has been increased by 250,000 more than usual. It has been necessary to make granaries into bedrooms; there is such a profusion of carriages that the streets are choked up with them, and many persons run great danger.

Some ladies of quality seeing a well-dressed woman covered with diamonds, and whom nobody knew, alight from a very handsome carriage, were curious to know who it was, and sent to enquire of the lackey. He replied, with a sneer, "It is a lady who has recently tumbled from a garret into this carriage." This lady was probably of the same sort as Madame Bejon's cook. That lady, being at the opera, some days back, saw a person in a costly dress, and decorated with a great quantity of jewels, but very ugly, enter the theatre.

The daughter said, "Mamma, unless I am very much deceived, that lady so dressed out is Mary, our cook-maid."

"Hold your tongue, my dear," said the mother, "and don't talk such nonsense."

Some of the young people, who were in the amphitheatre, began to cry out,
"Mary, the cook-maid! Mary, the cook-maid!"

The lady in the fine dress rose and said, "Yes, madam, I am Mary, the cook-maid; I have gained some money in the Rue de Quincampoix; I like to be well-dressed; I have bought some fine gowns, and I have paid for them. Can you say so much for your own?"

Mr. Law is not the only person who has bought magnificent jewels and extensive estates. The Duke, too, has become immensely rich, as well as all those who have held stock. Mr. Law has made his abjuration at Melun; he has embraced the Catholic religion, with his children, and his wife is in utter despair at it.

> [The abjuration did not take place at Paris, because the jokes of the Parisians were to be dreaded. The Abbe Tencin was so fortunate as to have the office of converting Mr. Law. "He gained by this pious labour," says Duclos, "a large sum in bank-notes and stock."]

It is amusing enough to see how the people run after him in crowds only to be looked at by him or his son. He has had a terrible quarrel with the Prince de Conti, who wished Mr. Law to do at the bank a thing which my son had forbidden. The Prince de Conti said to Mr. Law, "Do you know who I am?"

"Yes, Prince," replied Law, "or I should not treat you as I have done."

"Then," said the Prince, "you ought to obey me."

"I will obey you," replied Law, "when you shall be Regent;" and he withdrew.

The Princesse de Leon would be taken to the bank, and made her footmen cry out, "Room for the Princesse de Lion." At the same time she, who is very little, slipped into the place where the bankers and their clerks were sitting.

"I want some stock," said she.

The clerk replied, "You must have patience, madame, the certificates are delivered in rotation, and you must wait until those who applied before you are served."

At the same time he opened the drawer where the stock-papers were kept; the Princess snatched at them; the clerk tried to prevent her, and a fight ensued. The clerk was now alarmed at having beaten a lady of quality, and ran out to ask the servants who the Princesse de Leon was. One of the footmen-said, "She is a lady of high rank, young and beautiful."

"Well, then," said the clerk, "it cannot be she."

Another footman said, "The Princesse de Leon is a little woman with a hunch before and another behind, and with arms so long that they nearly reach the ground."

"Then," replied the clerk, "that is she."

Mr. Law is not avaricious; he gives away large soma in charity, and assists many indigent people.

When my son wanted some Duchess to accompany my daughter to Geneva, some one, who heard him speaking about it, said, "if, Monsieur, you would like to select from a number of Duchesses, send to Mr. Law's; you will find them all there."

Lord Stair cannot conceal his hatred of Mr. Law, and yet he has gained at least three millions by him.

Mr. Law's son was to have danced in the King's ballet, but he has been attacked by the small-pox (9th Feb., 1720).

....

My son has been obliged to displace Mr. Law. This person, who was formerly worshipped like a god, is now not sure of his life; it is astonishing how greatly terrified he is. He is no longer Comptroller-General, but continues to hold the place of Director-General of the Bank and of the East India Company; certain members of the Parliamentary Council have, however, been joined with him to watch over the business of the Bank.

> [In the Council of the Regency, the Duc d'Orleans was obliged to: admit that Law issued papers to the amount of 1,200 millions above the legal sum; and that he (the Regent) had protected him from all responsibility by decrees of the Council which had been ante-dated. The total, amount of bank-notes in circulation was 2,700,000,000 livres.]

His friend, the Duc d'Antin wanted to get the place of Director.

The Duke at first spoke strongly against Law; but it is said that a sum of four millions, three of which went to him and one to Madame de Prie, has engaged him to undertake Law's defence. My son is not timid, although he is threatened on all sides, and is very much amused with Law's terrors (25th June, 1720).

At length the latter is somewhat recovered, and continues to be great friends with the Duke: this is very pleasant to the Duc de Conti, and makes him behave so strangely that his infirmity is observed by the people. It is fortunate for us that Law is so great a coward, otherwise he would be very troublesome to my son, who, learning that he was joining in a cabal against him, told his wife of it. "Well, Monsieur," said she, "what would you have him do? He likes to be talked of, and he has no other way of accomplishing it. What would people have to say of him if he did not?"

On the 17th of June, while I was at the Carmelites, Madame de Chateau-Thiers came to me in my chamber, and said, "M. de Simiane is just come in from the Palais Royal, and he thinks it fit you should know that upon your return you will find the court of the Palais Royal filled with people, who, though they do not say anything, will not disperse."

At six o'clock this morning they brought in three dead bodies, which M.
Le Blanc ordered to be carried away immediately.

Mr. Law has taken refuge in the Palais Royal. The populace have done him no harm, but his coachman has been pelted on his return, and the carriage broken to pieces. It was the coachman's own fault, who said aloud that the people were rabble, and ought to be all hanged. I saw immediately that it would not do to display any fear, and I set off. There was such a stoppage of the carriages that I was obliged to wait half an hour before I could get into the Palais Royal. During this time I heard the people talking; they said nothing against my son, and bestowed benedictions upon me, but they all wished Law to be hanged. When I reached the Palais Royal all was calm again; my son came to me immediately, and, notwithstanding the alarm I had felt, he made me laugh; as for himself, he had not the least fear. He told me that the first president had made a good impromptu upon this affair. Having occasion to go down into the court, he heard what the people had done with Law's carriage, and, upon returning to the Salon, he said with great gravity:

> "Messieurs, bonne nouvelle,
> Le carrosse de Law est en canelle."

Is not this a becoming jest for such serious personages? M. Le Blanc went into the midst of the people with great firmness, and made a speech to them; he afterwards had Law escorted home and all became tranquil.

It is almost impossible that Law should escape, for the same soldiers who protect him from the fury of the people will not permit him to go out of their hands. He is by no means at his ease, and yet I think the people do not now intend to pursue him any farther, for they have begun to make all kinds of songs about him.

Law is said to be in such an agony of fear that he has not been able to venture to my son's at Saint Cloud, although he sent a carriage to fetch him. He is a dead man; he is as pale as a sheet, and it is said can never get over his last panic. The people's hatred of the Duke arises from his being the friend of Law, whose children he carried to Saint Maur, where they are to remain.

M. Boursel, passing through the Rue Saint Antoine in his way from the Jesuits' College, had his carriage stopped by a hackney coachman, who would neither come on nor go back. M. Boursel's footman, enraged at his obstinacy, struck the coachman, and, M. Boursel getting out of his coach to restrain his servant's rage, the coachman resolved to be avenged of both master and man, and so began to cry out, "Here is Law going to kill me; fall upon him."

The people immediately ran with staves and stones, and attacked Boursel, who took refuge in the church of the Jesuits. He was pursued even to the altar, where he found a little door opened which led into the convent. He rushed through and shut it after him, by which means he saved his life.

M. de Chiverni, the tutor of the Duc de Chartres, was going into the Palais Royal in a chair, when a child about eight years old cried out, "There goes Law!" and the people immediately assembled. M. Chiverni, who is a little, meagre-faced, ugly old man, said pleasantly enough, "I knew very well I had nothing to fear when I should show them my face and figure."

As soon as they saw him they suffered him to get quietly into his chair and to enter the gates of the palace.

On the 10th of December (1720), Law withdrew; he is now at one of his estates about six miles from Paris. The Duke, who wished to visit him, thought proper to take Mdlle. de Prie's post-chaise, and put his footman into a grey livery, otherwise the people would have known and have maltreated him.

Law is gone to Brussels; Madame de Prie lent him her chaise. When he returned it, he wrote thanking her, and at the same time sent her a ring worth 100,000 livres. The Duke provided him with relays, and made four of his own people accompany him. When he took leave of my son, Law said to him, "Monsieur, I have committed several great faults, but they are merely such as are incident to humanity; you will find neither malice nor dishonesty in my conduct." His wife would not go away until she had paid all their debts; he owed to his rotisseur alone 10,000 livres.

> [Mr. Law retired to Venice, and there ended his
> days. Some memoirs state that he was not married
> to the Englishwoman who passed for his wife.]